VOL. 17

HAL•LEONARD®

HARMONICA PLAY•ALONG

AUDIO ACCESS INCLUDED

MUDDY WATERS

CONTENTS

PLAYBACK+
Speed • Pitch • Balance • Loop

To access audio visit:
www.halleonard.com/mylibrary
Enter Code
8604-7545-2673-3510

Steve Cohen: Harmonica
Billy Flynn and Kirk Tatnall: Guitar
Marc Wilson and Eric Hervey: Bass
Dave Kasik and Dave Schoepke: Drums

Cover photo © Getty Images / Paul Natkin

T0056509

ISBN 978-1-4584-3204-9

HAL•LEONARD®

Visit Hal Leonard Online at
www.halleonard.com

Contact Us:
Hal Leonard
7777 West Bluemound Road
Milwaukee, WI 53213
Email: info@halleonard.com

In Europe, contact:
Hal Leonard Europe Limited
42 Wigmore Street
Marylebone, London, W1U 2RN
Email: info@halleonardeurope.com

In Australia contact:
Hal Leonard Australia Pty. Ltd.
4 Lentara Court
Cheltenham, Victoria, 3192 Australia
Email: info@halleonard.com.au

Blow, Wind, Blow

Words and Music by McKinley Morganfield

Verse

1. Well, __ when the sun rose this morn - in',

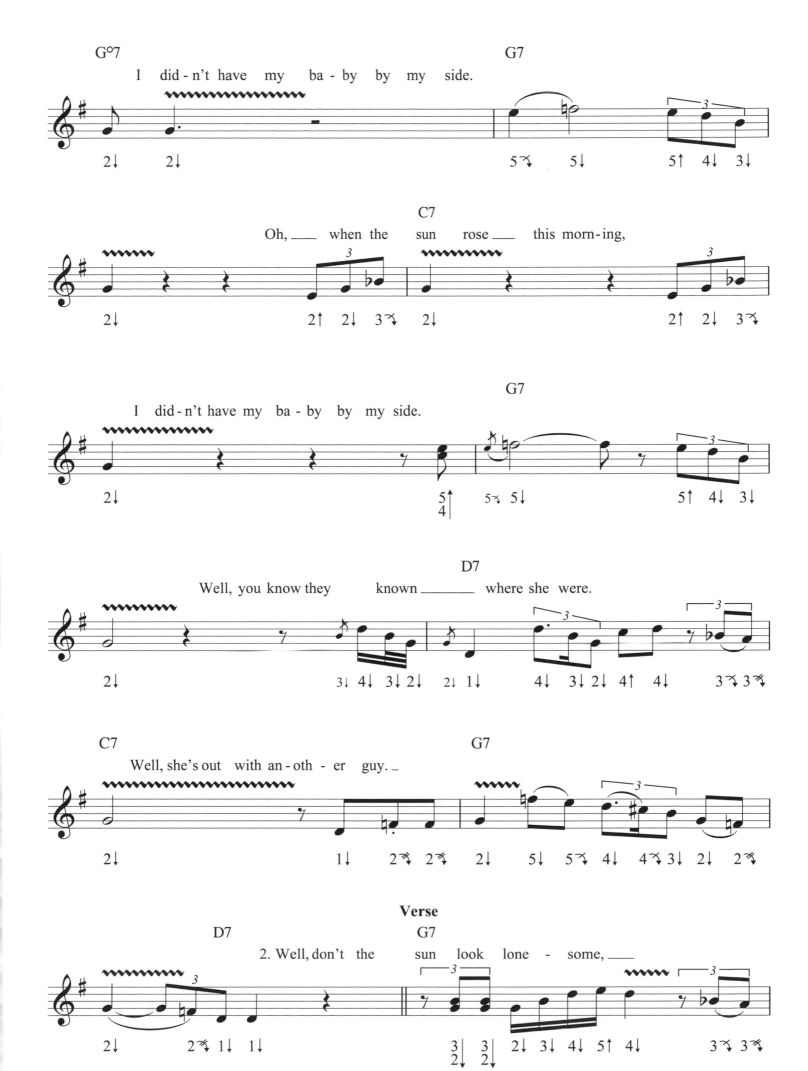

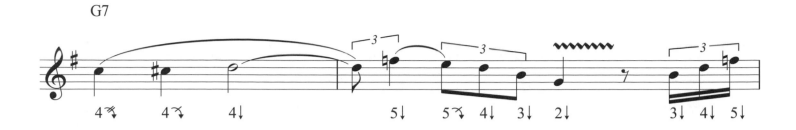

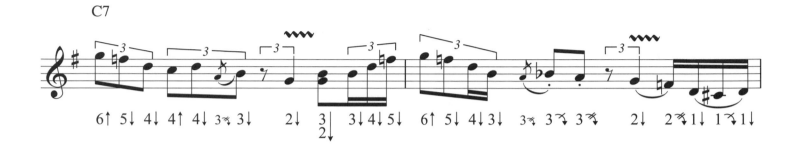

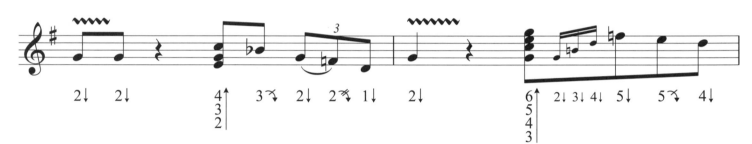

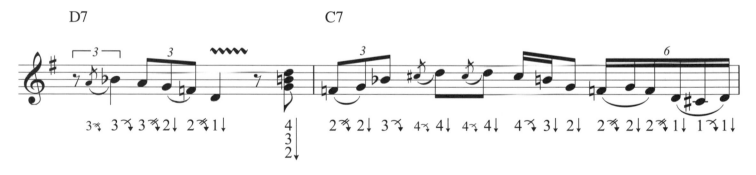

3. Oh,

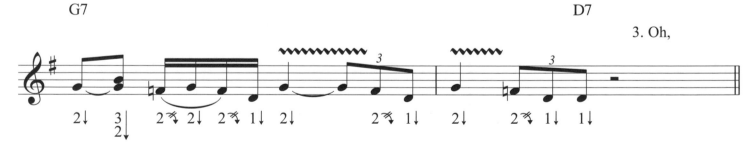

Verse

G7

blow   wind, blow   wind, ___   blow   my   ba - by back to   me.

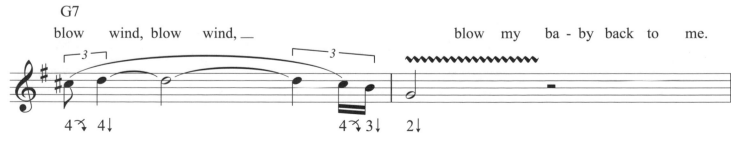

5

Oh,

4↷ 4↓   4↷ 3↓ 2↓   2↓   3↓ 4↓ 5↓ 6↓ 6↑ 5↓ 4↓ 4↑ 3↓ 2↓ 2↷ 2↓ 2↷

C7

blow wind, blow wind,   blow my ba - by back to me.

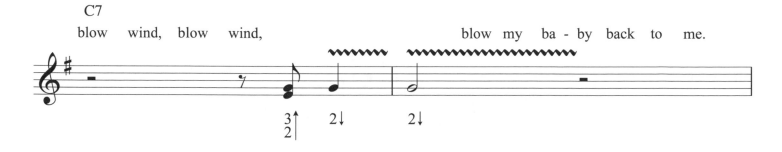

3↑ 2↓   2↓
2

G7

Well, you know if I

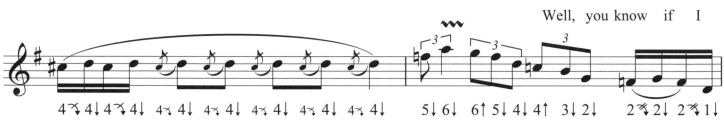

4↷ 4↓ 4↷ 4↓   4↷ 4↓   4↷ 4↓   4↷ 4↓   4↷ 4↓   4↷ 4↓   5↓ 6↓   6↑ 5↓ 4↓ 4↑   3↓ 2↓   2↷ 2↓ 2↷ 1↓

D7   **C7**

don't soon find her,   my heart's gon - na be in mis-er - y.   Well

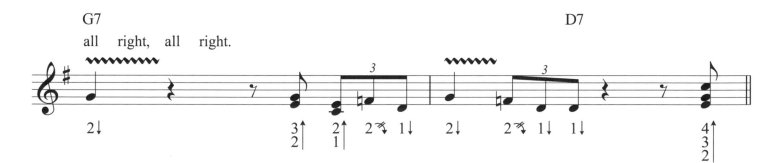

3↑ 2↷ 2↓ 2↷ 2↓ 2↷ 1↓   2↓   3↑   2↷ 2↓ 2↷ 1↓
2   2

G7   **D7**

all right, all right.

2↓   3↑   2↑   2↷ 1↓   2↓   2↷ 1↓ 1↓   4↑
                    2   1   3
                                                                                  2

Piano Solo

     G7

2↓ 2↓ 3↷ 3↓ 2↓ 2↓ 2↷ 1↓ 1↷ 1↓   2↓ 2↓ 3↷ 3↓ 2↓   5↑ 3↓   2↓ 2↓ 3↷ 3↓ 2↓ 2↓ 2↷ 1↓ 1↷ 1↓
                                                                4↑ 2
                                                               3

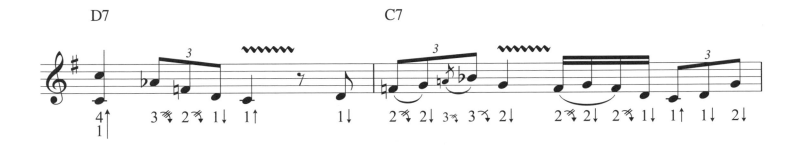

Verse

G7

good - bye   ba - by.

G°7

I   don't have   no more to say.

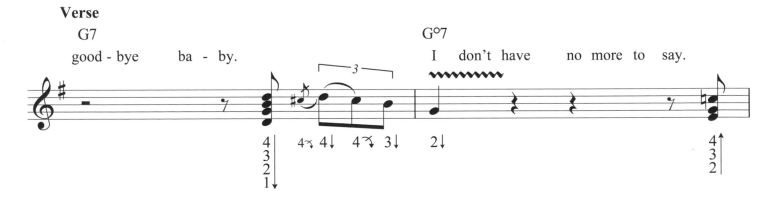

G7

Oh,

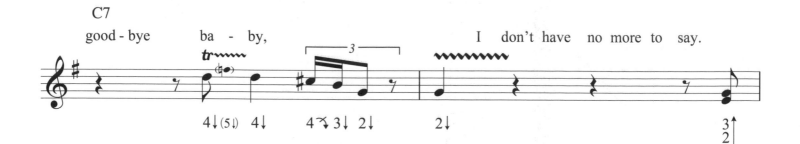

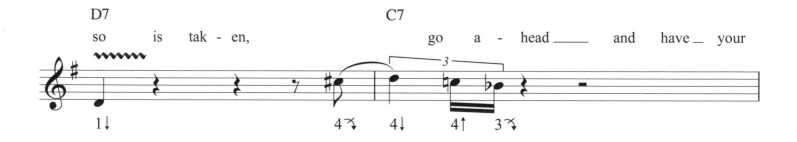

Louisiana Blues

Words and Music by McKinley Morganfield

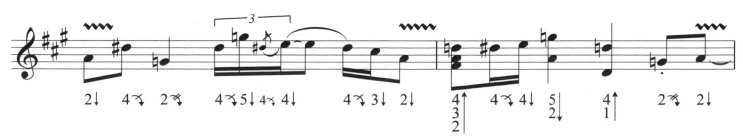

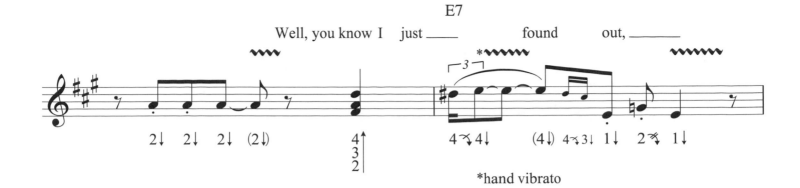

E7

Well, you know I just _____ found out, _____

*hand vibrato

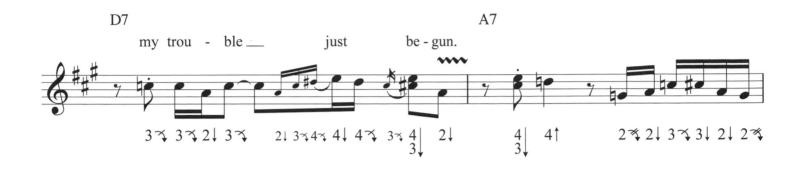

D7   A7

my trou - ble ___ just be - gun.

2. I'm go - in' down to

Verse

D7

New Or - leans, mm, get me a ____ mo - jo hand. _

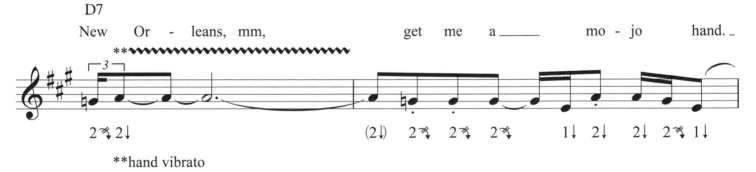

**hand vibrato

A7

_____

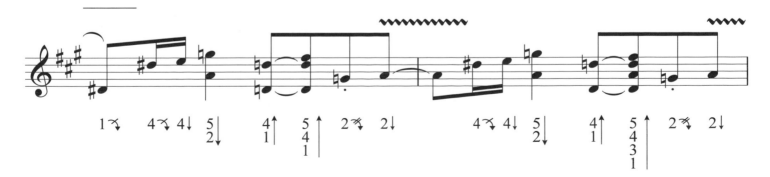

D7

I'm goin' down in New Or - leans,

*hand vibrato

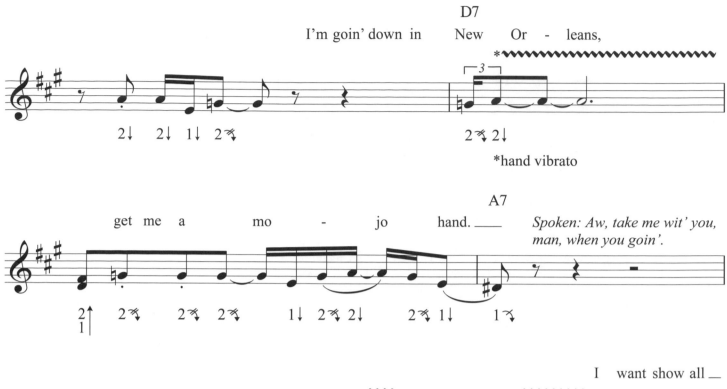

2↓ 2↓ 1↓ 2↗   2↗ 2↓

A7

get me a mo - jo hand. ____ *Spoken: Aw, take me wit' you, man, when you goin'.*

2↑ 2↗ 2↗ 2↗ 1↓ 2↓ 2↓ 2↗ 1↓ 1↗
1↑

I want show all __

4↗ 4↓ 5↓ 5↑ 3↓ 2↓ 1↓ 2↗ 2↗ 2↓   2↓ 2↓ 2↓
2↓   4
        3↑

E7   D7

__ you good look-in' woman   just how to __ treat your man.

4↗4↓   4↗3↗2↓ 1↓   2↗2↗2↗1↓   3↗ 3↗3↗2↓3↗   2↓3↗ 4↗ 4↓ 3↗ 3↗ 2↓

A7

4↓ 4↑ 2↗ 2↓ 3↗ 3↓ 2↓   1↓ 2↓ 3↓ 4↑ 2↗ 2↓ 3↗ 3↓ 2↓
3↓

Harmonica Solo

D7

2↓ 2↓ 2↓ (2↓)   2↗ 2↓   3↗ 3↓ 2↓ (2↓)

**hand vibrato

12

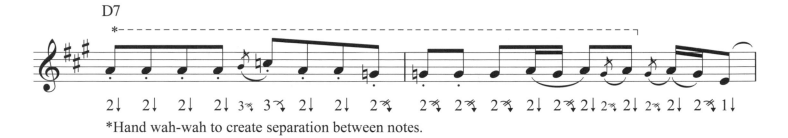

*Hand wah-wah to create separation between notes.

**hand vibrato

Forty Days and Forty Nights

Words and Music by Bernard Roth

HARMONICA

Harp Key: D Diatonic

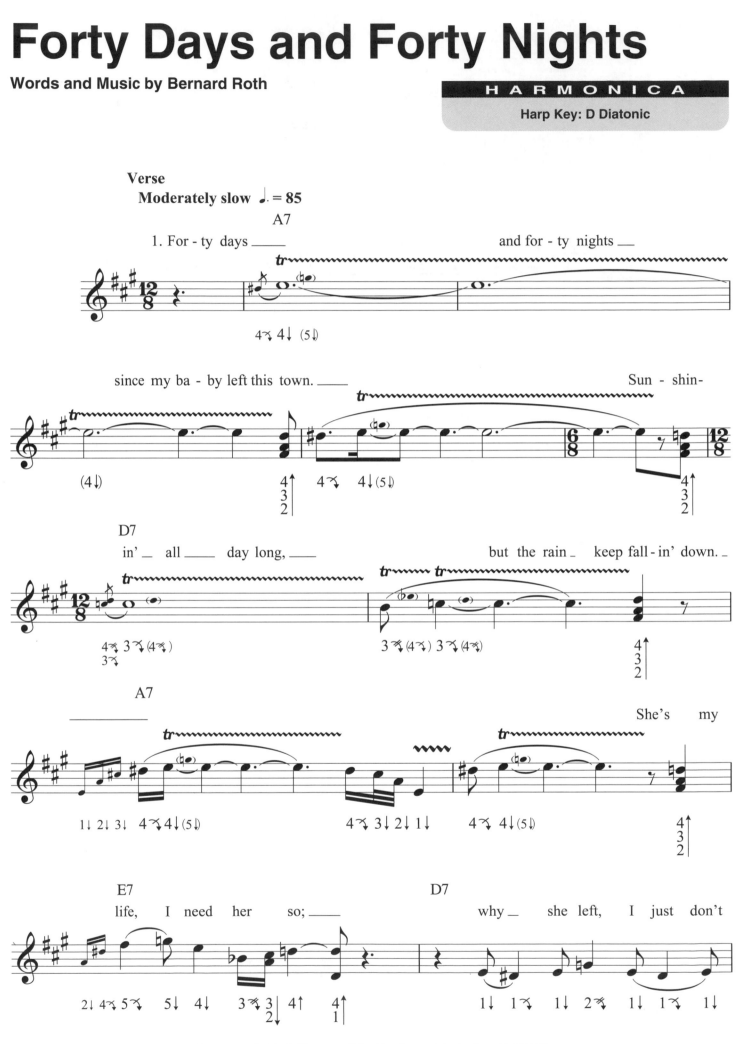

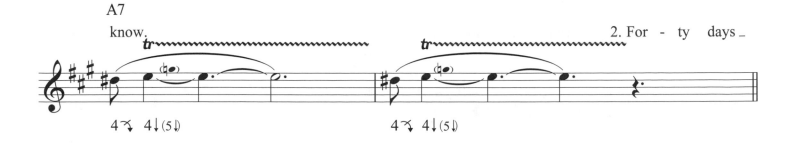

Verse

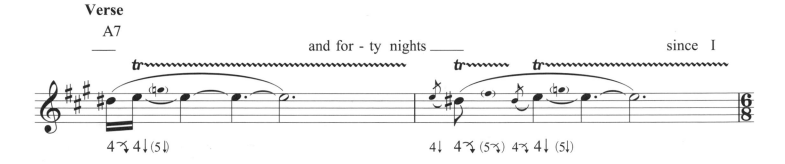

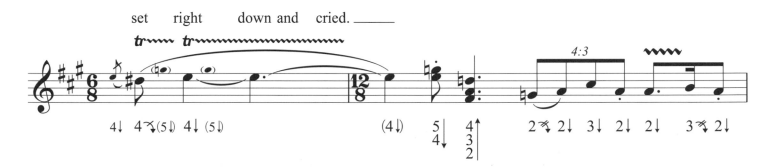

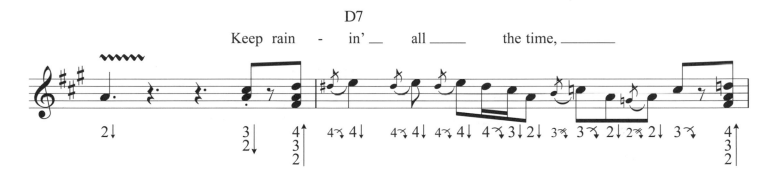

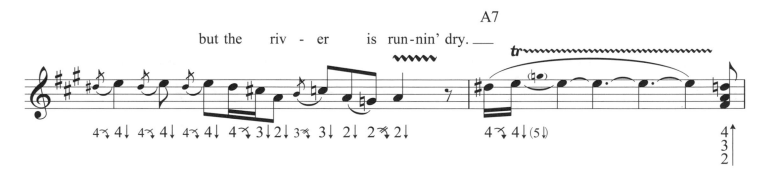

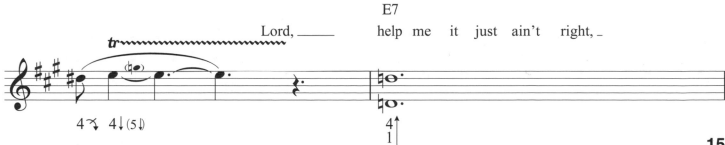

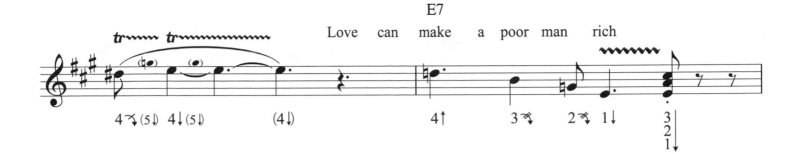

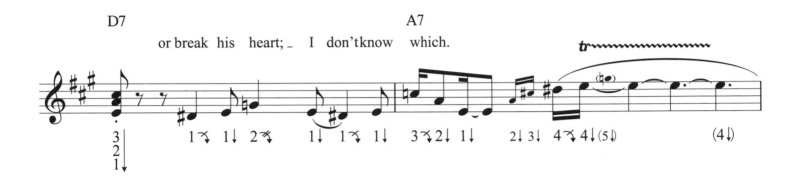

Harmonica Solo

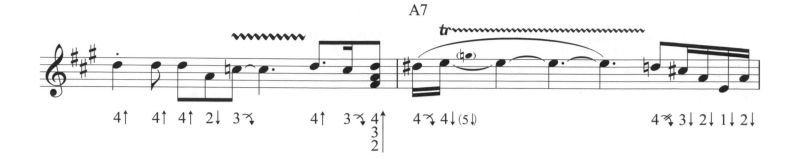

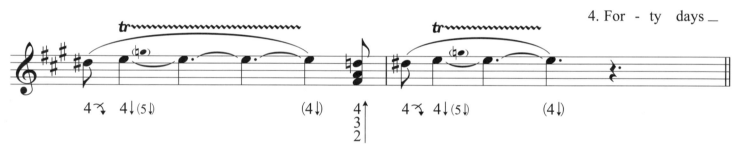

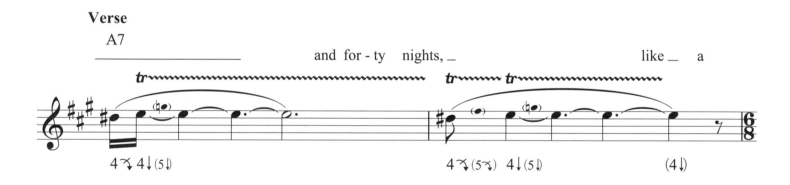

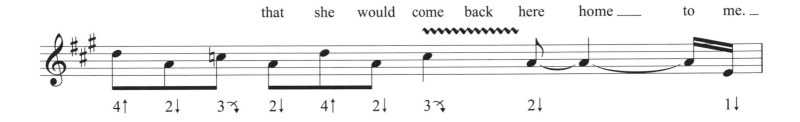

Good Morning Little Schoolgirl

Words and Music by Willie Williamson

HARMONICA

Harp Key: D Diatonic

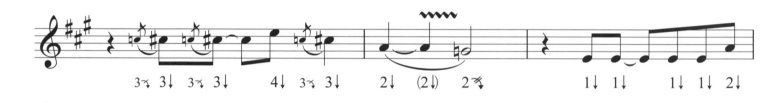

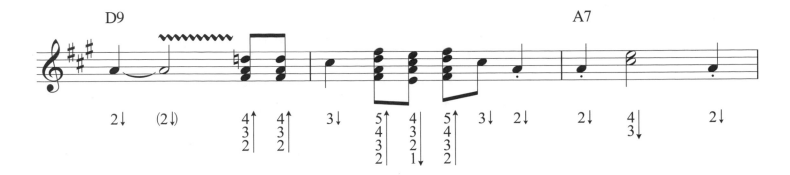

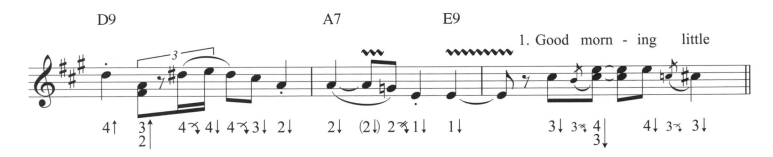

Verse

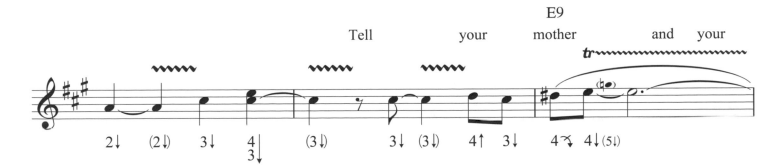

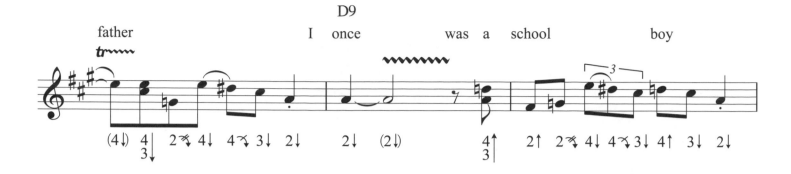

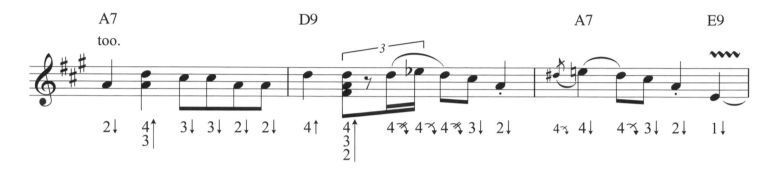

Guitar Solo

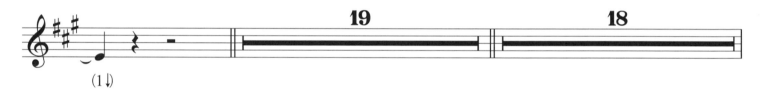

Verse

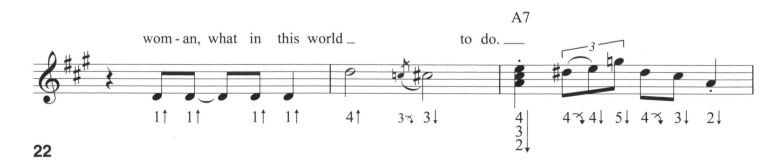

You know I don't wanna

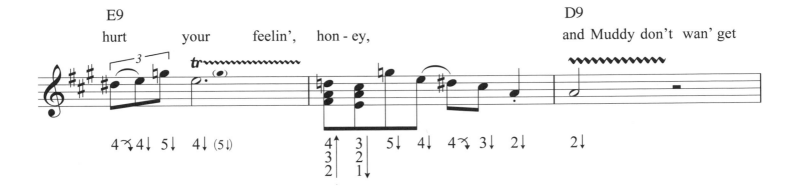

hurt your feelin', hon-ey,

E9

and Muddy don't wan' get

D9

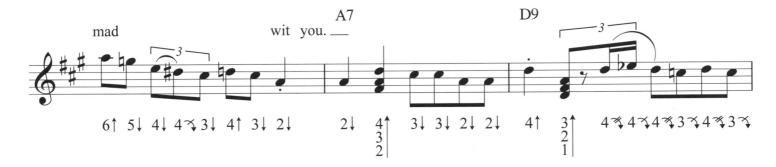

mad

wit you. ___

A7

D9

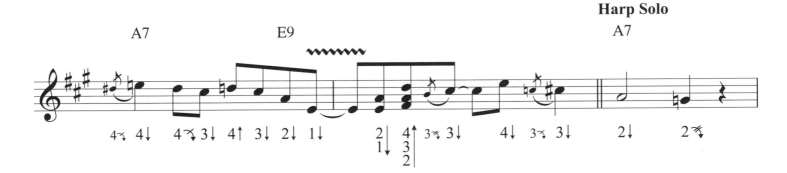

Harp Solo

A7

E9

A7

D9

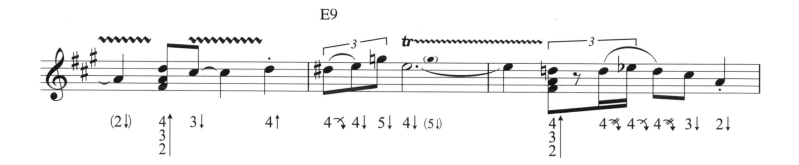

Verse

A7

3. I'm   gon - na buy   me a   air - plane,   I'm gon - na buy   me a

Mannish Boy

Words and Music by McKinley Morganfield, Melvin London and Ellas McDaniel

HARMONICA

Harp Key: D Diatonic

I'm a man. ___   I'm a roll - in' stone. _

2↓   3↑ 4↑ 3↑ 3↘ 3↓   2↓   3↑ 4↑ 3↑ 3↘ 3↓

I'm a man. __   I'm a hooch-ie cooch-ie man.

2↓   3↑ 4↑ 3↑ 3↘ 3↓ 2↓   3↑ 4↑ 3↑ 3↘ 3↓

Verse

A

2. Sit -tin' on the out - side,   just me and my mate,

2↓   3↑ 4↑ 3↑ 3↘ 3↓   2↓   3↑ 4↑ 3↑ 3↘ 3↓

you know I made the moon, hon- ey,   come up two hours late.

2↓   3↑ 4↑3↑ 3↘ 3↓ 2↓   5 | 3↑ 4↑3↑ 3↘ 3↓
                                                                 4↓

Chorus

A

Was - n't that a man?   I spell "M," _

2↓   3↑ 4↑ 3↑ 3↘ 3↓   2↓   3↑ 4↑ 3↑ 3↘ 3↓

"A," __   child,   "N," __

2↓   3↑ 4↑ 3↑ 3↘ 3↓   2↓   3↑ 4↑ 3↑ 3↘ 3↓

that rep-re-sent man.　　　　　　No "B,"

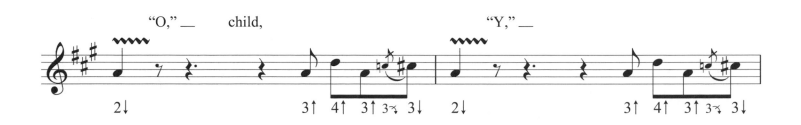

"O," — 　　child,　　　　　　"Y," —

that mean man-nish boy.　　　　　　Man, ___

I'm a full-grown man.　　　　　　Man, ___

I'm a nat-'ral-born lov-er's man.　　　　　　Man, ___

I'm a roll - in' stone.　　　　　　Man _ child, _

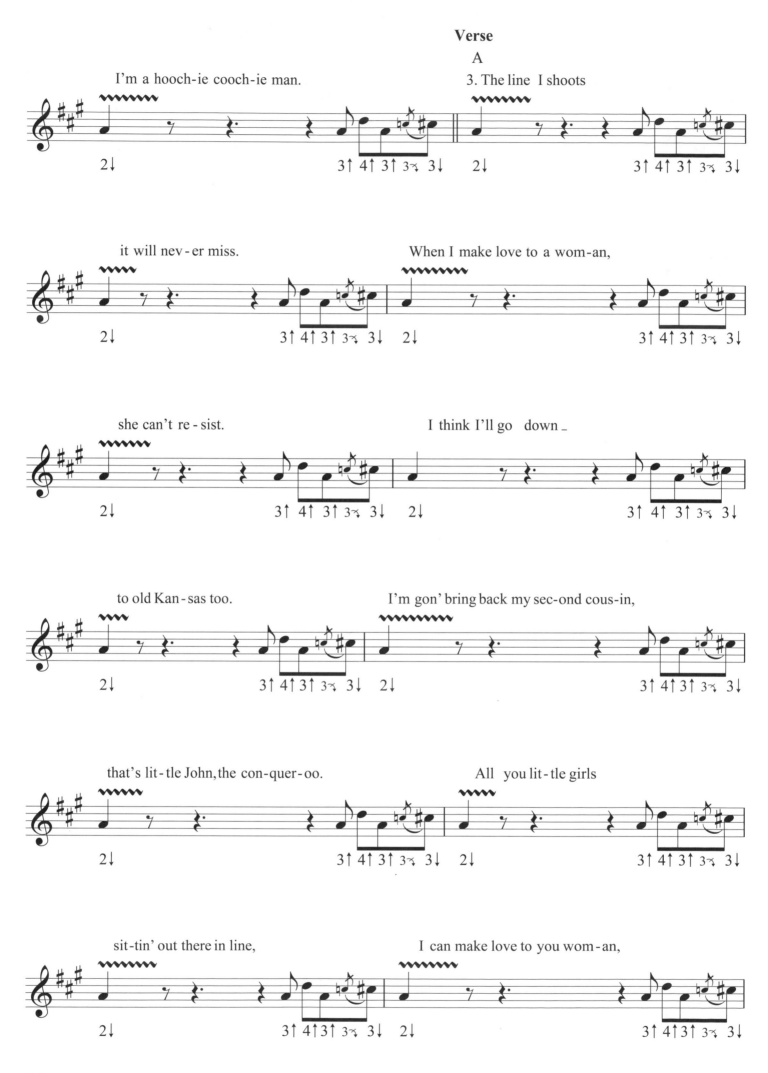

Chorus

A

in five min-utes time.   Ain't that a man?

I spell "M,"   "A," __ child, _

"N," __   that rep-re-sent I'm grown.

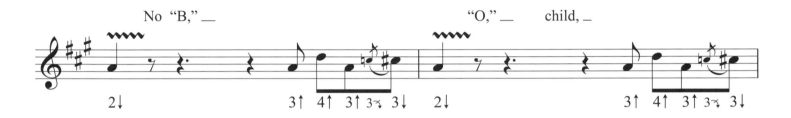

No "B," __   "O," __ child, _

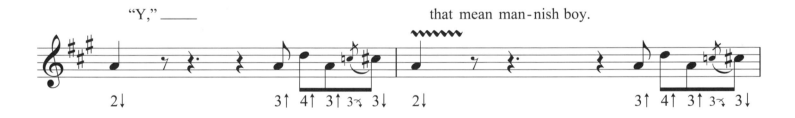

"Y," ____   that mean man-nish boy.

Man, _____   I'm a full-grown man.

Man, _   I'm a nat-'ral-born lov-er's man.

Standing Around Crying

Words and Music by McKinley Morganfield

HARMONICA

Harp Key: B♭ Diatonic

Verse

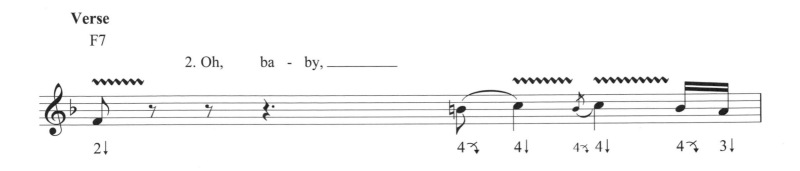

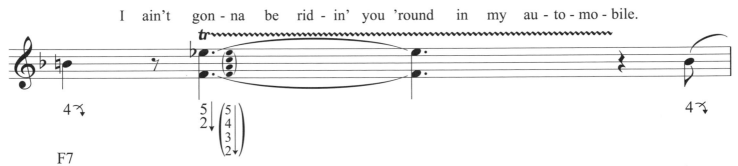

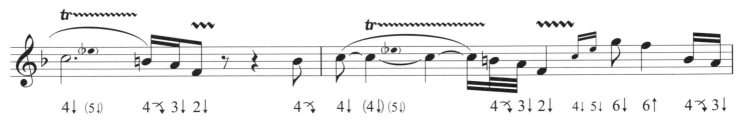

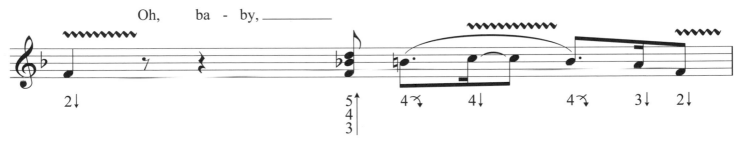

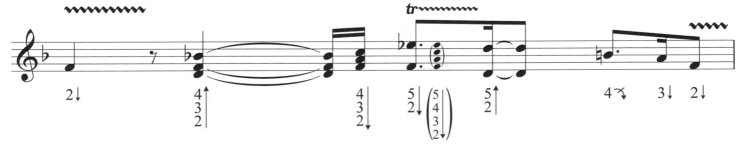

Verse

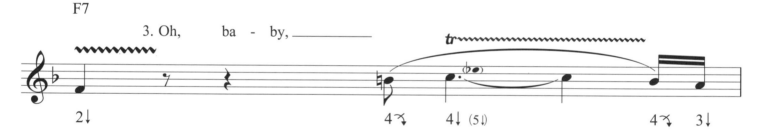

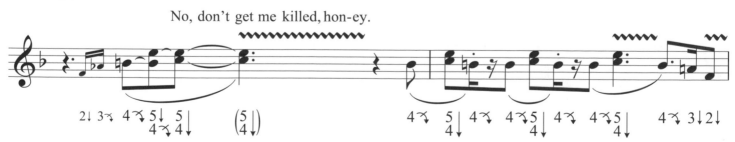

Walking Through the Park

Words and Music by McKinley Morganfield

H A R M O N I C A

Harp Key: A Diatonic

Intro
Moderately ♩ = 134

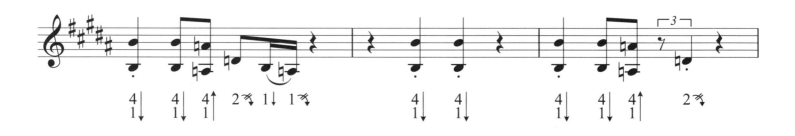

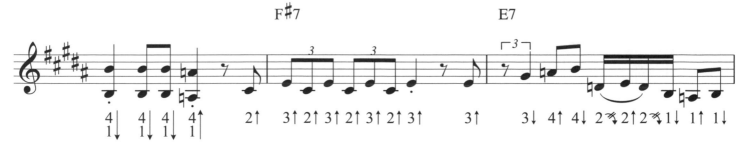

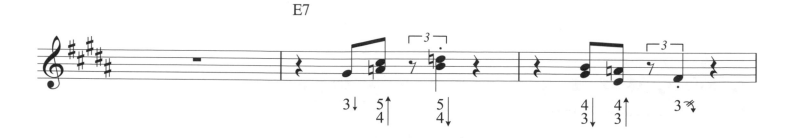

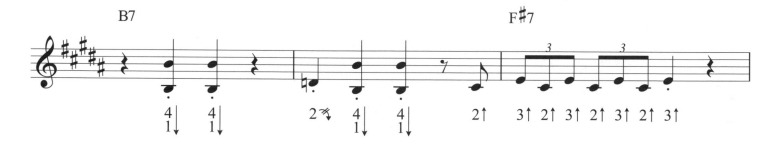

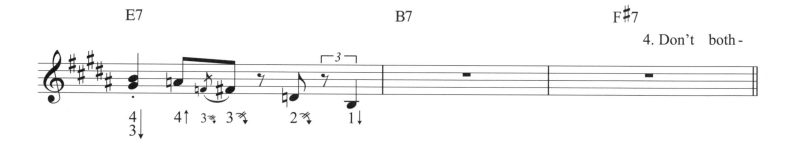

Verse

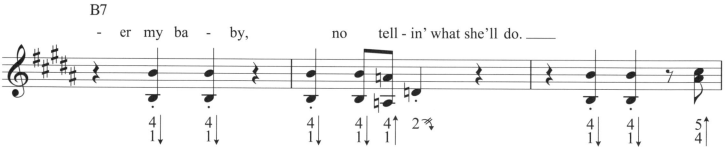

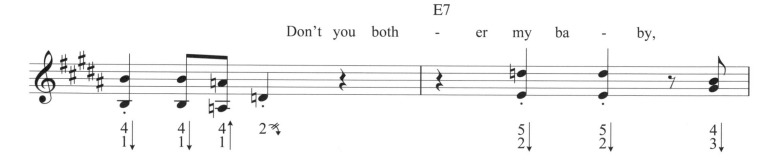

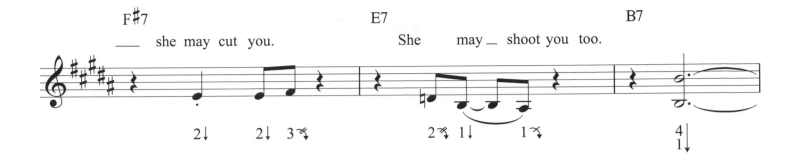

she may cut you.　　　She　　may＿ shoot you too.

Outro

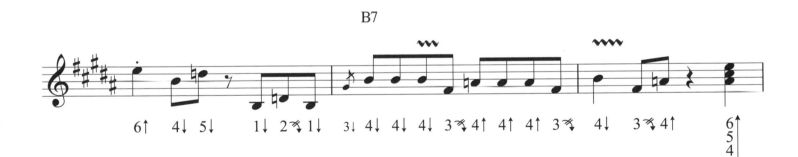

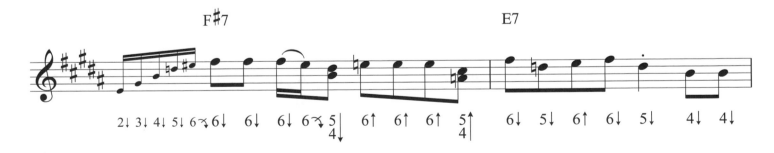

Free time

Trouble No More
(Someday Baby)

Words and Music by McKinley Morganfield

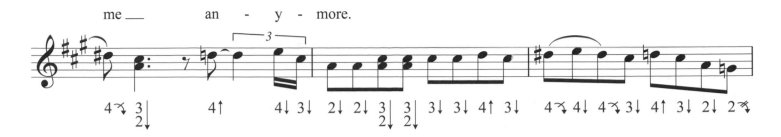

Verse

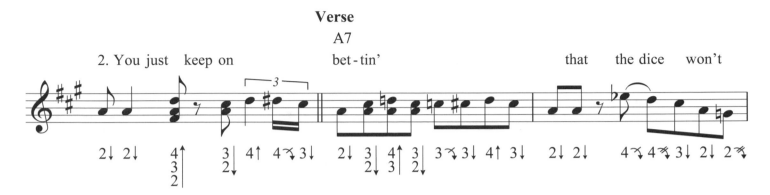

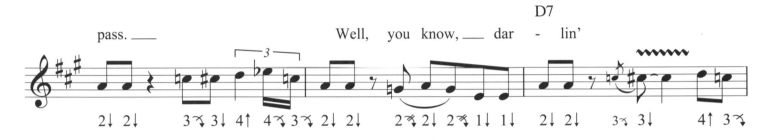

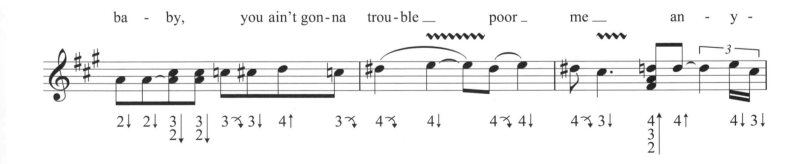

Verse

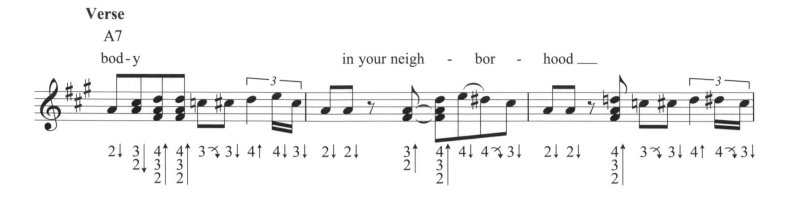

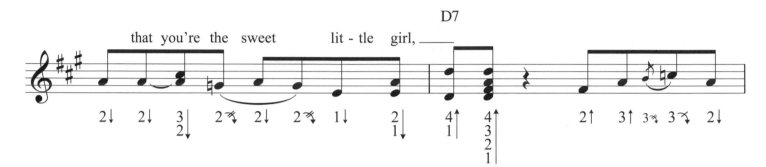

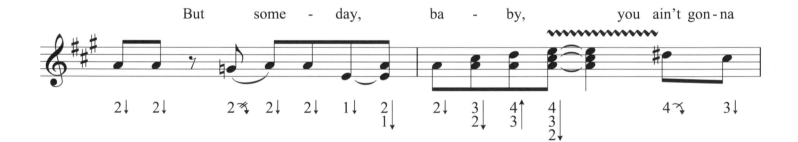

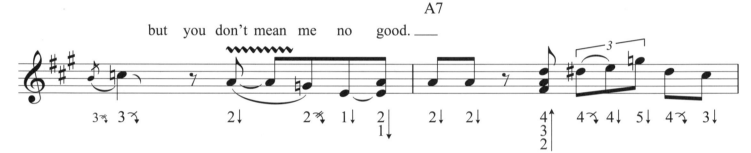

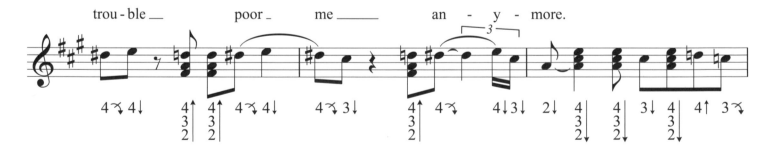

Harmonica Solo

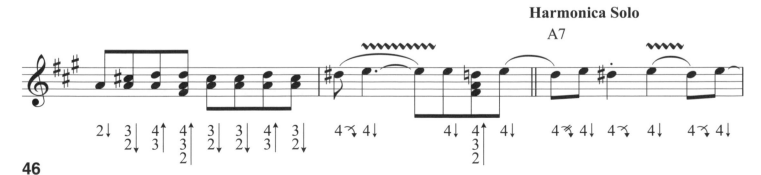

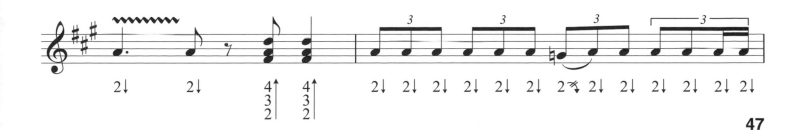

D7

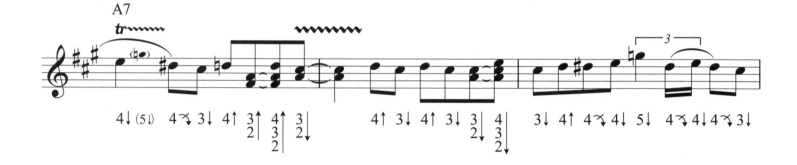

A7

Guitar Solo

A7

48

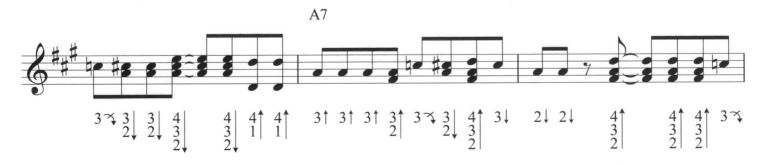

4. I'm gon-na tell ev - 'ry-

Verse

A7

bod - y   in your neigh - bor - hood _____

D7

that you're a sweet lit - tle girl, _____

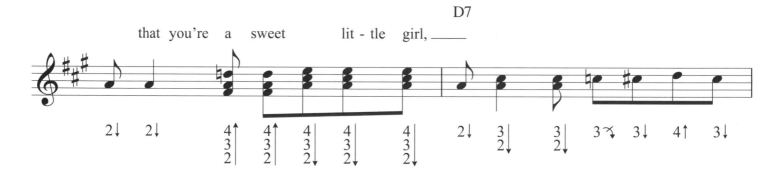

A7

but you don't mean me no good. __

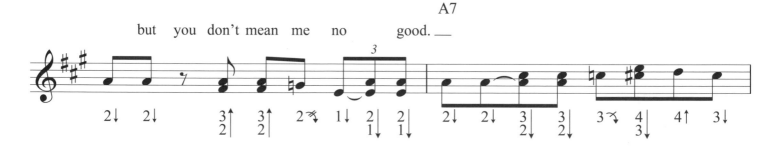

But some - day, ba - by, you ain't gon - na

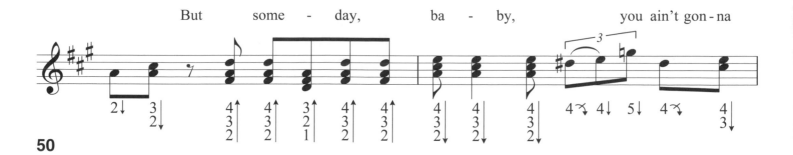

50

Verse

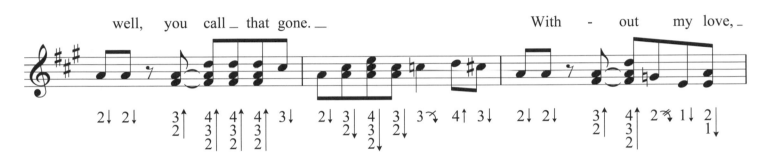

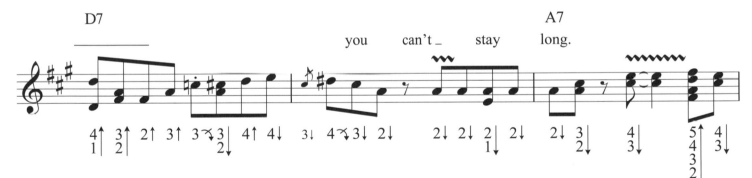

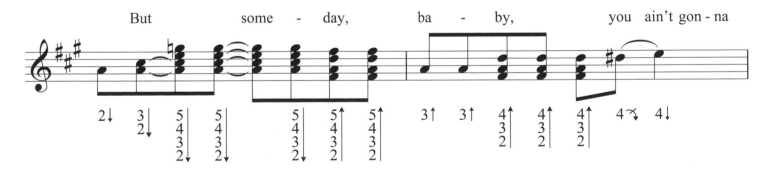

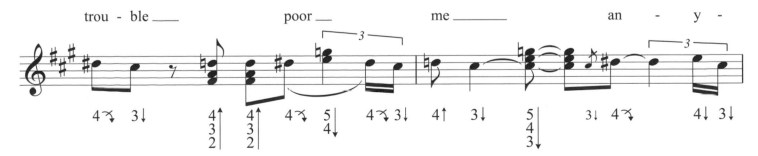

Verse

A7

D7

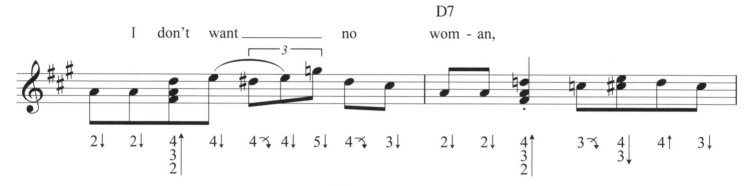

A7

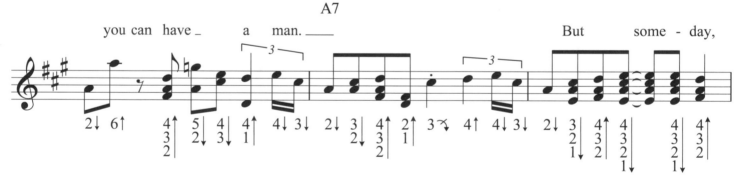

*tongue-blocking tremolo

HARMONICA NOTATION LEGEND

Harmonica music can be notated two different ways: on a *musical staff*, and in *tablature*.

THE MUSICAL STAFF shows pitches and rhythms and is divided by bar lines into measures. Pitches are named after the first seven letters of the alphabet.

TABLATURE graphically represents the harmonica music. Each note will be accompanied by a number, 1 through 10, indicating what hole you are to play. The arrow that follows indicates whether to blow or draw. (All examples are shown using a C diatonic harmonica.)

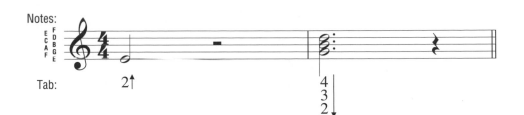

Blow (exhale) into 2nd hole.

Draw (inhale) 2nd, 3rd, & 4th holes together.

Notes on the C Harmonica

Exhaled (Blown) Notes

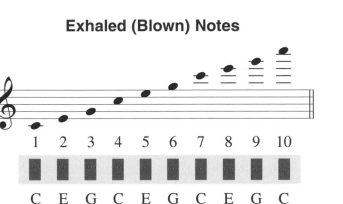

Inhaled (Drawn) Notes

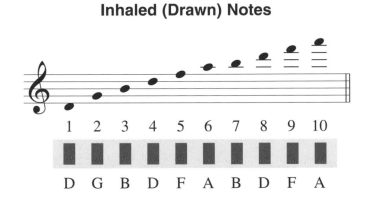

Bends

Blow Bends

↗	• 1/4 step
	• 1/2 step
	• 1 step
	• 1 1/2 steps

Draw Bends

↘	• 1/4 step
	• 1/2 step
	• 1 step
	• 1 1/2 steps

Definitions for Special Harmonica Notation

SLURRED BEND: Play (draw) 3rd hole, then bend the note down one whole step.

GRACE NOTE BEND: Starting with a pre-bent note, immediately release bend to the target note.

VIBRATO: Begin adding vibrato to the sustained note on beat 3.

TONGUE BLOCKING: Using your tongue to block holes 2 & 3, play octaves on holes 1 & 4.

TRILL: Shake the harmonica rapidly to alternate between notes.

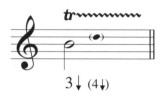

NOTE: Tablature numbers in parentheses are used when:

- The note is sustained, but a new articulation begins (such as vibrato), or
- The quantity of notes being sustained changes, or
- A change in dynamics (volume) occurs.
- It's the alternate note in a trill.

Additional Musical Definitions

D.S. al Coda
- Go back to the sign (𝄋), then play until the measure marked "**_To Coda_**," then skip to the section labelled "**Coda**."

D.C. al Fine
- Go back to the beginning of the song and play until the measure marked "**_Fine_**" (end).

- Repeat measures between signs.

(accent)
- Accentuate the note (play initial attack louder).

(staccato)
- Play the note short.

1. 2.
- When a repeated section has different endings, play the first ending only the first time and the second ending only the second time.

Dynamics

_p_
- Piano (soft)

_mp_
- Mezzo Piano (medium soft)

_mf_
- Mezzo Forte (medium loud)

_f_
- Forte (loud)

(crescendo)
- Gradually louder

(decrescendo)
- Gradually softer

HAL•LEONARD® HARMONICA PLAY-ALONG

AUDIO ACCESS INCLUDED

Play your favorite songs quickly and easily!

Just follow the notation, listen to the audio to hear how the harmonica should sound, and then play along using the separate full-band backing tracks. The melody and lyrics are also included in the book in case you want to sing, or to simply help you follow along. The audio CD is playable on any CD player. For PC and Mac computer users, the CD is enhanced so you can adjust the recording to any tempo without changing pitch!

1. Pop/Rock
And When I Die • Bright Side of the Road • I Should Have Known Better • Low Rider • Miss You • Piano Man • Take the Long Way Home • You Don't Know How It Feels.
00000478..$14.99

2. Rock Hits
Cowboy • Hand in My Pocket • Karma Chameleon • Middle of the Road • Run Around • Smokin' in the Boys Room • Train in Vain • What I like About You.
00000479..$14.99

3. Blues/Rock
Big Ten Inch Record • On the Road Again • Roadhouse Blues • Rollin' and Tumblin' • Train Kept A-Rollin' • Train, Train • Waitin' for the Bus • You Shook Me.
00000481..$14.99

4. Folk/Rock
Blowin' in the Wind • Catch the Wind • Daydream • Eve of Destruction • Me and Bobby McGee • Mr. Tambourine Man • Pastures of Plenty.
00000482..$14.99

5. Country Classics
Blue Bayou • Don't Tell Me Your Troubles • He Stopped Loving Her Today • Honky Tonk Blues • If You've Got the Money (I've Got the Time) • The Only Daddy That Will Walk the Line • Orange Blossom Special • Whiskey River.
00001004..$14.99

6. Country Hits
Ain't Goin' down ('Til the Sun Comes Up) • Drive (For Daddy Gene) • Getcha Some • Here's a Quarter (Call Someone Who Cares) • Honkytonk U • One More Last Chance • Put Yourself in My Shoes • Turn It Loose.
00001013..$14.99

8. Pop Classics
Bluesette • Cherry Pink and Apple Blossom White • From Me to You • Love Me Do • Midnight Cowboy • Moon River • Peg O' My Heart • A Rainy Night in Georgia.
00001090..$14.99

9. Chicago Blues
Blues with a Feeling • Easy • Got My Mo Jo Working • Help Me • I Ain't Got You • Juke • Messin' with the Kid.
00001091..$14.99

10. Blues Classics
Baby, Scratch My Back • Eyesight to the Blind • Good Morning Little Schoolgirl • Honest I Do • I'm Your Hoochie Coochie Man • My Babe • Ride and Roll • Sweet Home Chicago.
00001093..$15.99

HAL•LEONARD®
Visit Hal Leonard Online
at **www.halleonard.com**

Prices, content, and availability subject to change without notice.

11. Christmas Carols
Angels We Have Heard on High • Away in a Manger • Deck the Hall • The First Noel • Go, Tell It on the Mountain • Jingle Bells • Joy to the World • O Little Town of Bethlehem.
00001296..$12.99

12. Bob Dylan
All Along the Watchtower • Blowin' in the Wind • It Ain't Me Babe • Just like a Woman • Mr. Tambourine Man • Shelter from the Storm • Tangled up in Blue • The Times They Are A-Changin'.
00001326 ....$16.99

13. Little Walter
Can't Hold Out Much Longer • Crazy Legs • I Got to Go • Last Night • Mean Old World • Rocker • Sad Hours • You're So Fine.
00001334 ....$14.99

14. Jazz Standards
Autumn Leaves • Georgia on My Mind • Lullaby of Birdland • Meditation (Meditacao) • My Funny Valentine • Satin Doll • Some Day My Prince Will Come • What a Wonderful World.
00001335..$16.99

15. Jazz Classics
All Blues • Au Privave • Comin' Home Baby • Song for My Father • Sugar • Sunny • Take Five • Work Song.
00001336 ....$14.99

16. Christmas Favorites
Blue Christmas • Frosty the Snow Man • Here Comes Santa Claus (Right down Santa Claus Lane) • Jingle-Bell Rock • Nuttin' for Christmas • Rudolph the Red-Nosed Reindeer • Santa Claus Is Comin' to Town • Silver Bells.
00001350..$14.99